Jaid & Jax. My life
is better because of you!
Love Mommy (G.B)

To my awesome superhero, Xavier.
You are my inspiration.
Love Dad (S.A.J)

for
Jax and Jaid and Xavi

FIRST EDITION
10 9 8 7 6 5 4 3 2 1

strangerkids.com
Stranger Kids is a division of Stranger Comics

Stranger Comics | Los Angeles, CA

Sometimes we all need little
reminders of what makes us special, unique
and awesome. Growing up and throughout life, we all must
find our place in the world, and that journey is different for each of
us. For some of us, our parents and friends encourage our dreams, while
others discover their paths through trial and error. As a child, imagination is
the greatest source of inspiration we have, and it gives us the sense that "all
dreams are possible." As an adult, that is easy to forget. The *I Am Awesome* book
embraces the idea that each and every one of us is Awesome and helps reinforce
some of the most important values in life for parent and child alike. Being good at
soccer or math is great, but so is being brave, being a good friend, and never giving up.

I Am Awesome celebrates the innocent journey
of self-discovery through imagination and
creative wonder, and THAT is awesome.

– Angie Harmon

i am
AWESOME

written by
Garcelle Beauvais & Sebastian A. Jones

illustrated by
James C. Webster

art direction & storyboards
Darrell May

concept art
James C. Webster - Darrell May - Davida Benefield - Paul Davey

design & production art
Adrienne Sangastiano

editorial
Joshua Cozine

I am awesome at being a superhero.

Like

Look at me, Mom, I can leap over the couch.

I said watch this, Mommy, I'm no slouch.

I can run faster than a rocket or train.
And if I fall, I get up, and I do it again.

Are you watching? I never give up.

i am awesome.

I am awesome at being brave.

Like

When the light goes click, I hear creaking doors.

But there are no monsters that creep on all fours.

No creatures or ghosts that go bump in the night.
But if there were, I'd hug them with all of my might.

Squeeze! I am not afraid of the dark.

i am awesome.

I am awesome at playing games.

Like

I've nearly finished, Dad...

We must beat this level or be totally lame.

We've done our homework and raked all the leaves.
Finished our chores and played make believe.

I've got the highest score! I always try my best.

i **am** awesome.

I am awesome at being a friend.

Like

Nia and I jump rope at our school.

One foot, hop, we are so cool.

With Ravi, I share my favorite toy.
Teaching Spanish to Jay is such a great joy.

Best friends forever! I always have fun.

i am awesome.

i am so awesome, one day I'll be King.
President or Queen, or some marvelous thing.

For now, I'll be awesome at being me.

I fence with my foil and fool all my foes.

I conjure tricks in tuxedos and bows.

I dance on my tip toes in tutus of pink.

I ride on my bike as quick as a wink.

I rock the triangle in the school band.

I can draw dragons with my left hand.

I stand up for my pals when they are teased.

I love being adopted. My parents chose me.

i am awesome

just like YOU.

Tell us what makes you
AWESOME too!

Everyone in the world is different and every single person is **AWESOME!** One of life's greatest joys is discovering what you are good at and all of the things that you enjoy. Have fun learning about yourself and celebrate the things that make you YOU because YOU are AWESOME!

about me...

My name is _____ .

I am _____ years old.

I have _____ brother(s) and _____ sister(s).

I live in _____ .

My favorite thing to do is _____ .

My favorite song is _____ .

My favorite food is _____ .

My best friends are _____ .

If I could have any super power it would be _____ .

I am AWESOME because _____

_____

_____ !

DRAW YOUR SUPERHERO:

My super power is...

DRAW SOMETHING AWESOME:

i am...

A note for parents:

After sharing *I Am Awesome* with your child, you can use these discussion questions to start a conversation about what your child enjoys and what makes him/her unique. Make sure you tell your child the things that make them special to you! This can help reinforce confidence and celebrate how your child is AWESOME!

1. What does it mean to be awesome at something? Who is your hero and what makes them awesome?

2. When Nia falls down and gets back up, she doesn't give up. Why is trying again a good thing?

3. Lenore is awesome at being brave. What does it mean to be brave? What are some ways that you are brave?

4. Why does Sally's dad want her to do her chores before homework? What are your favorite indoor and outdoor games?

5. Why is it important to be a good friend like Gabriel? What can you do to be a better friend?

6. Think about our family. What makes each person in our family awesome?

7. What makes YOU awesome?

STRANGER
K I D S

See more from the *I Am* book series and other great titles.

 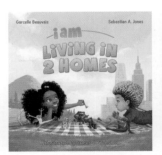 

strangerkids.com

Originally from England, **Sebastian** founded the critically acclaimed MVP records at 18, turning his love of American roots music into a business. More recently, he created Stranger Comics to do the same with his love of fanciful tales and quality escapism. Sebastian is honored to celebrate the *I Am* book series with his son, Xavier.

Stranger Comics
educational director
Megan Lewitin
marketing
Eddie DeAngelini
Hannibal Tabu
Tabitha Grace Smith
development
Mike Hodge
Christopher Garner
digital supervisor
Ken Locsmandi
art director
Darrell May
editor-in-chief
Joshua Cozine
publisher
Sebastian A. Jones

Born to create, **James** is a menagerie of artistic expression, interpretation and execution. Classically trained by an array of talented professors at Syracuse University, James has been working with the Stranger team since 2011. He currently resides in Atlanta with his extremely talented and brilliant lady, Adrienne, the designer and production artist for the *I Am* book series.

Garcelle is Haitian born and immigrated to the United States at the age of seven. She has since charmed audiences with her dramatic and comedic abilities in both television and film. Always wanting to give back, Garcelle is active with charities including Step  Up Women's Network, March of Dimes, and EDEYO, a Haitian children's organization. In addition to writing children's books, she has a popular blog on People.com focusing on parenting and all things women. Garcelle lives in Los Angeles, where she is happiest spending time with her sons, Oliver and the twins, Jax and Jaid, who were the inspiration for the series.

We would like to thank

Paul Almond, TC Badalato, Marie Beaubien, Marie Claire Beauvais, The Bergtings, Kami Broyles, Andrew Cosby, Elena Cunningham, Dawn Eyers, Jennifer Foutch, Kristina Gravely, Jennifer Green, Mark & Katie Hammond, Mark Hovanec, Gray Jones, Noel Johnson, Lloyd Levin, Bob Lieberman, Mona Loring, Norma McCandless, Kristen Merlene, Omilaju Miranda, Craig Pollock, Indira Salazar, Oliver Saunders, Diane Simowski, Sonia Smith-Kang, Dr. Sophy, Andrew Sugerman, Tim Taylor, Rose Tinker, Lori-Ann & Jens Quast, Elizabeth Ricin, David Uslan and Luke Whitehead